Crow Feathers

i

DEDICATION

To all the people we have lost, especially Colin Daisy.

As a mark of respect, readers are asked not to use his first name in public, but 'old man', 'uncle' or 'kumanjay' instead.

Crow Feathers

My granma's hands
are brown as muddy water
she come from Cummergunga way.
She lost a son, she lost her youngest daughter
When they took the children away.

My granma's eyes
are dark as stormy weather
she make a damper everyday.
The ties that bind are severed now forever
She cry a little anyway.

My granpa's skin
is blacker than the shadders
he's from Hopkins River way.
He went to war to fight off the invaders;
they were here already anyway.

My granpa's hands
are blacker than the midnight
he worked hard everyday
for truth, respect and equal rights.
He got less than equal pay.

My granparents
are black as two crow feathers.
I am proud of who they are today.
They fought to live and love and die together
in the country that belongs to them anyway.

John Lewis Clark

1

Gorgeous George

Gorgeous George the gangster,
way past his prime.
Drooling on the verandah
reminiscing crime.
Wild women, cadillacs,
truckloads of booze.
The kiss of death
a gangster slap
a pair of cement shoes.

Gorgeous George the gangster
dribbling in his chair.
Losing all his good looks
lost most of his hair.
Grab a cloud punk!
Rat a tat tat!
You're the dirty brother
that killed my rat.

Gorgeous George the gangster
in striped pyjama suit
got twenty years for speeding
with a body in the boot.
Come and get me coppers
I'll fill yas full of lead!
Car chase. Shoot out.
The lights turned red.

Gorgeous George the gangster
fumbles in his vest
reaching for that ghostly gun
beside his bony chest.
Bang! Bang! Bang! Bang!
Smoking fingertip.
A desperado on the run
firing from the hip.

Gorgeous George the gangster
a relic from the past
when bad guys came first
good guys came last.
That's it George. Let 'em have it.
Squeeze the trigger. Pull it.
George ain't the same
since the day he became
a home for a single stray bullet.

John Lewis Clark

John Lewis Clark

3

Neon Atmosphere

I saw the dogs eat dog on the street last night.
I saw an angel in leather on a wicked black bike.
I saw a pig fly by with a flashing blue light.
I saw Stallone, De Niro, Brad Pitt lookalikes.

I saw a man kiss a man in the neon atmosphere.
I saw something queer
I saw a tongue in an ear.
I saw a good man drown in a glass of beer.
I saw a woman sell herself
I saw a sign: KEEP CLEAR.

I saw the pavement crack along the jungle track
I saw a queen with the jack
I saw the joker attack
I saw a knife in the back
I saw a junky blow his mind on the steel tram track.

I saw the mouths to feed on the streets of greed
I saw a friend with weed
I saw a desperate need
I saw them sow their seeds
I saw them hurt themselves
I saw them let it bleed

John Lewis Clark

This Great South Land

Have you ever crossed flooded rivers in an old Land Rover
    with water up to the bonnet?
Have you ever been so impressed with the Australian bush
    you had to write a sonnet?

Have you bathed in a small winding stream,
    or drank water from a trickling creek?
Have you basked in the beauty of the Australian bush
    and listened to nature speak?

Have you heard the orchestral sound of chanting cicadas,
    or listened to the hoot of a lone bush Owl?
Have you ever lain in bed late at night listening to
    the eerie sounds of a wild dingo's howl?

Have you smelt the freshness of eucalyptus leaves,
    and gazed upon the beauty of a tall gum tree?
Have you embraced the serenity of the Australian bush
    and loved its peace and harmony?

Have you collected fat little tadpoles from a rock pool,
    or held a tiny Penny Turtle in the palm of your hand?
Have you ever been camping out in the Australian bush
    and enjoyed the beauty of this Great South Land?

Marian Go Sam

The Storyteller

From the outback he came, with a strange sounding name -
Bujara, Buguya, or something very similar.
His grey hair hung long, his white beard hung longer.
He cared not how others saw him, his words just grew stronger.

He told all who would listen, all who came near,
Stories of courage stories of fear.
Stories of country, stories of creators,
The magic of wisdom, a gift from the makers.

His eyes would shine bright as he talked through the night,
By his campfire ashes with his swag rolled up tight.
As a pillow he used it for the night was not cold,
But, in the flickering flames, you could see he looked old.

He talked of his life as the spirits looked on.
He knew in his heart soon he too would be gone.
And as his ancestors waited he showed no fear
And held out his hand as they drew near.

To the old outback man I said my farewell.
He gave me one last story I am not ready to tell -
Of the place he was going to, where the journey would lead,
Instructions one day I know I will need.

I hear no more stories from that old outback man,
Though I see his face often, tell his stories when I can.
He gave me the wisdom, a gift from our past,
To take into the future, make our heritage last.

I tell those who will listen, those who show fear,
How our culture survives, why we hold it so dear.
Like the old outback man my eyes open wide,
His voice echoes through me, his spirit by my side.

His task was to carry these stories through life,
To give them meaning in sand with the blade of his knife.
I pass on these stories to children, women and men.
When others draw near, I will help you tell them.

K.athleen Davies

Kathleen Davies

7

8

Kathleen Davies

Listen and Learn

Have you heard it?
The creaking of the earth?
When it breathes
you can feel it.

It's the land
that you possess
that comes alive
when you are asleep.

You can hear it
when you are half-conscious
you can talk to it
when you are dreaming.

It can hear you
it can feel you
it can ignore you
it can deceive you.

It's an ancient being
that only contacts the wise
it holds secrets from the beginning of time.

But only the wise can hear it
and talk of its wisdom.
The ones who are loud
are too proud to listen.

9

Yunke

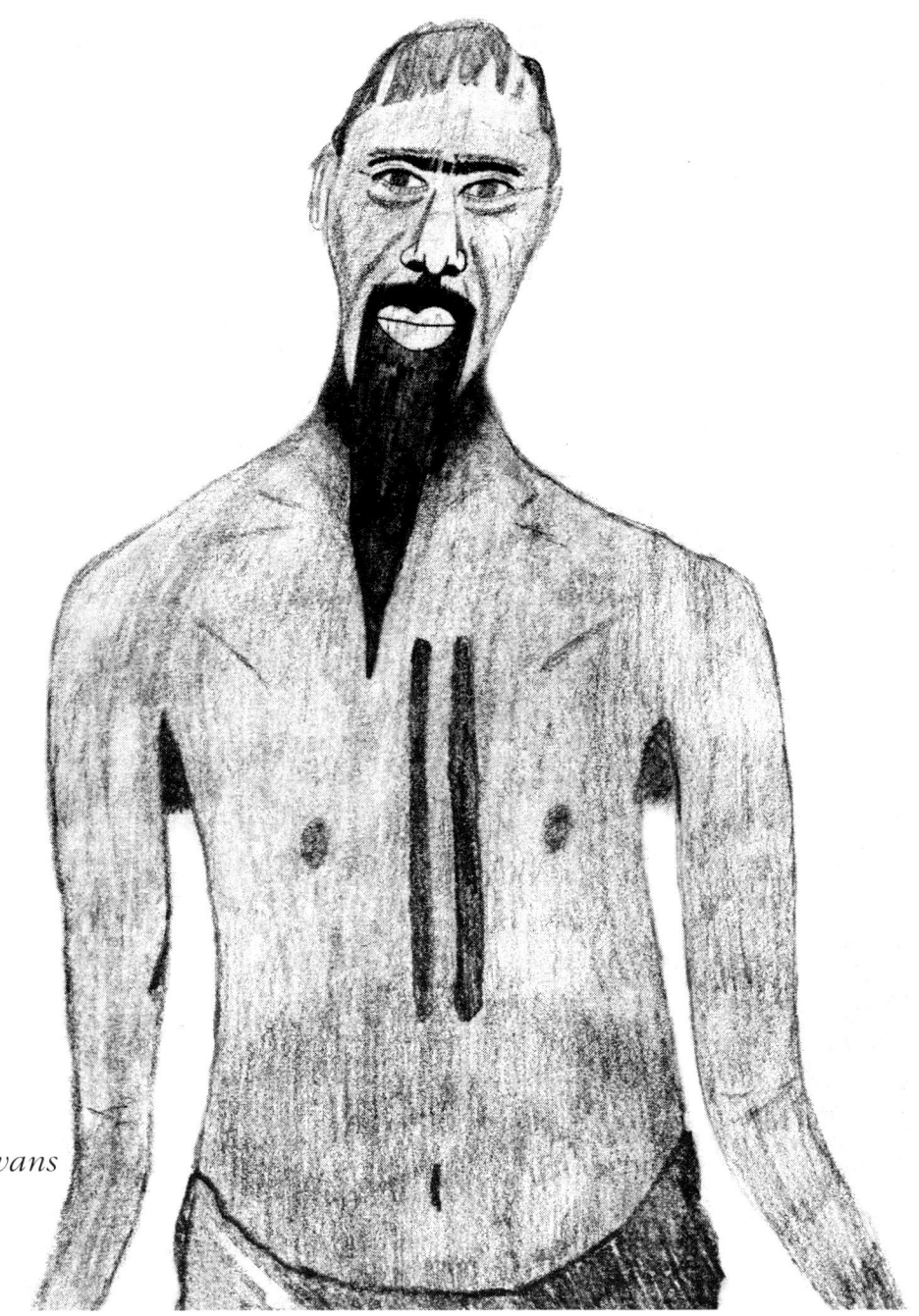

Janelle Evans

Come Back

Listen to the wind.
Listen to your heart.
The message is coming
the animals are silent
the trees that once stood proud and aloft
are now drooped and bowed.
The sun is hot
the clouds bring no rain
feel it in your heart
feel the pain.

This land that held a thousand stories
this night that heard a thousand songs
sadly go
passing by.

"Listen" the wind is saying
"Don't forget,
"don't let the culture die."
The sky is saying
"Come let the boomerangs fly!"
The land is begging,
begging to be danced upon.
"Come!" it is saying,
"Make me smile, make me feel grand."
The clouds wish to spread rain
wish to give life to the land.

The spirits are in your dreams
they're calling to your hearts
they're calling, calling!
"You're Aboriginal!
Your skin is fair,
your skin is black!"

They're calling, calling!
"The land needs you,"
they're calling, calling!
"Come back."

Lindsay Ohl

Lost

I gaze into the flames of the campfire
and finally understand the reasons why
she could not answer our questions
when we were children.

Already my life is half over
and I feel the same sadness fill my heart
when my teenage nephews with looks of anticipation
on this night ask in earnest of their cultural ancestry

as into the night we yarn
with the fire being fueled many times
I see the confusion amongst all
as I explain why things are as they are.

I drift back to an earlier time as they present their queries.
Could this be me asking my mother?
Who is our tribe?
What are our customs?
Do I have a totem? What's our bloodline or skin group?

As I dwell on the endless questions
that I asked so long ago
I let my mind wander and think out loud
only to be brought back to the present

as I hear one boy ask:
Uncle, why are there tears in your eyes?
And what do you mean when you say
they took grandma away?

Lindsay Ohl

13

Jaquanna Elliot

The Tallest Tree to Fall

No more the bushland rings to the sounds of long ago;
for men have left the country, and now the cities grow.
So far away from Nature we're moving every day;
someone sound the warning for the price that we shall pay.

But each one of us is thinking: "Let the next one bear the load.
"Is that not the law of nature, the ethics of a code?"
Soon man will pay most dearly a price beyond recall
as the damage we've inflicted, one day will reach us all.

So lift your eyes skyward, and thank the Lord on high
for man made in His image, He will not deny.
But still we keep destroying the richest gift of all;
the mind, the human body: the tallest tree to fall.

Ellen Go-Sam

Timelessness

Green grasses sweet and lush from summer rains
grew along the roadside.
Cloud rested on the mountaintop
shrouding the mysteries of the long ago
when her own dark people roamed at will.
Through the trees on the mountainside
voices echoed from the undergrowth
singing sweet the song of the seasons.
Murmuring waters crashing like dewdrops
washed clean the breath of the land.

Alone she stood bathed in golden sunlight
wrapped in its shining glory her heart sang
rejoicing in its loving embrace
like the dreams of the ancient ones
threading and weaving their mystical wisdom
through the caverns of her soul.

Fallen tears brushed her cheek.
Rich with the moisture of a thousand lifetimes
wandering into the forest of her dreaming
she sailed alone like the winds on an empty ocean.

Ellen Go-Sam

Lucky Country

Who owns this country?
Where do they come from?

Are they Australians?
Are they Poms?

What did they bring here?
What do they speak?

Do they speak English?
Do they speak Greek?

They bring trouble.
They bring guns.

Shoot you dead
You nothing but a bum.

They say you're a no hoper
You no good.

You just nothing
You're just a boong

Where can we go?
Where can we stay?

Stand up and fight
Kneel down and pray.

We have to do something
We have to together

We can't do it alone
We can make it better

So, come on you people
Let's come as one

Bring you family
Children, Dad and Mum

Bring all your friends
Bring all relations

This is what we call!
Reconciliation.

Dennis Fisher

Behind a Smile

Today I saw a friend of mine sitting alone. I can see he was
far away, thinking of the love he left behind. So sad to see the pain
he hides. But what can he do. He gave his life to this jail, and let
his past be forgotten for now.

The sound of a love song recalls the time he held his sweet girl in his arms.
The memory of her face, her body holds him in thought for a while.

He stands up, looks around, then walks away. In his mind the
sound of "Not today, not today," brings him back to this day to find
he is still in jail.

Colin Daisy

Jaquanna Elliot

Mistake

Australia, named by the whiteman
explored by the whiteman
claimed by the whiteman.

The land of the dark skin people
for centuries they have walked this land,
lived with the land, called the earth mother,
a spiritual land, a land for the free of spirit.

For centuries my race has walked every coast line,
through valleys, across plains and deserts,
across this country we now call Australia.

I have read books on how the whiteman
discovered and named everything he could see
and reach across this land.

What a fool, the land has been named long before he came.
Here blackman has lived in this land
long before Adam and Eve were made.

The books I have read in school
tell how whiteman took land and killed my race
made it his home and called my ancestors savages,
uncivilised black bastards!

Over two hundred years before the whiteman came
my ancestors had no shame
they lived in harmony with the land.

Today we walk with our heads bent low,
we carry the shame the whiteman gave to us.

He walks with his head in the air; too shame
to look down and see his shame looking up at him:
head of his clan, John Howard;
too shame to say sorry for his ancestors.

My ancestors walk in the bye and bye with no shame
as they have before the whiteman came,
free spirit, free to walk the land of the black people
and creators of this spiritual country.

Colin Daisy

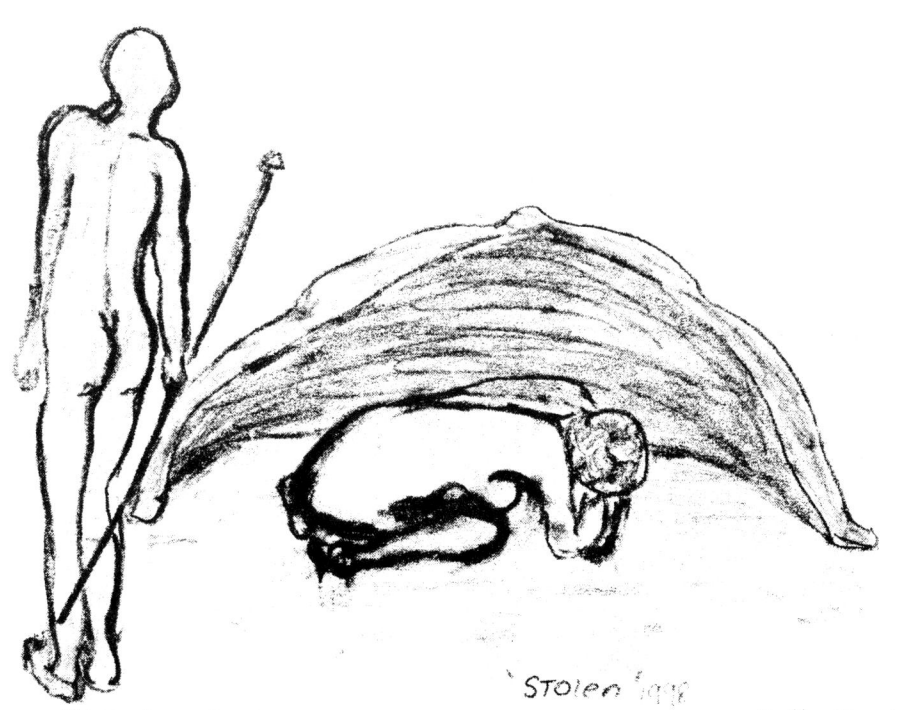

'STOLEN' 1998

Sally Davis

Cry

My race are the black people of the land where man first
walked the earth.
We are the first people in the book of our Lord
and according to the Book we are the last to stand up for our
rights and to be accepted as people of the land.
Our life has always been a hard one.
We lived with the land and called it mother.
Our father lived in the sky and looked down on his people
and said: this land and the people can take care of themselves.

I have seen my blood flow from the black skin of my body.
I have seen my brother shot dead.
I have seen my sister raped and bashed to the ground and
our mother the earth soak up the blood.
I have seen the fire that killed the children and consumed
the souls from their bodies.
I have seen the look of hate
and it came over the sea with the white sails
to the land of the hunters and gatherers.

I have seen death take the life of my people with long
knives that reached into their bodies.
Oh! How I cried for the loss of their souls.
Oh! How I cried for babies of the land.
Oh! How I cry for my Black race!
Oh! How I cried!
Oh! How I cry, Oh! I cry!

Colin Daisy

Old Man Cassowary

The cassowary cries for his rainforest home.
From Bloomfield to Daintree where his ancestors roam
farmers and graziers invaded their land
pushed down their food trees, condongs and yams.
He walks through the forest, with stealth and grace
wondering about his future, his children, and his place.

White man came with guns and dogs
cut down his forest, timbers and logs.
The tears rolled down from his big brown eyes
as he watched his forest cut down to size.
They cleared his land for cattle to graze
not thinking of him, or what they made

He lived on this land since Time began
and shared the rainforest with his tribal clans.
He lived so peacefully with his people back then
singing and dancing, again and again.

Malcolm Bally

Kathleen Davies

Bindi

Mother Earth.

You say you care for Mother Earth
her sky, her waters, her land.
With sad eyes I see the destruction
when will you make a stand?

We all know the need for clean water
on it all life depends
But if the sea dies and the rivers run dry
it's not something you can mend

Don't think the desert is useless
there lives the goanna, the snake;
Mother Earth was not made just for you
each creature, each plant has its place.

Conserve the scrub and the wallum
of this you may not be aware
it's the home of the roo and the possum;
they die if the land is made bare

Treat with respect the rain forest
leave it and let it grow tall
a little of Mother Earth will perish
each time a native tree falls

Make sure you care for all children
they are the future you see
I see the hunger, the bruises, the tears
this isn't the way it should be

So go back to the old ones, the elders
respect their stories and lore
learn from their wisdom and knowledge
repeat not mistakes made before.

Now is the time to consider
the things we do that are wrong
the prejudice, violence, destruction and lies
we must leave these things and go on

Now is the time for decisions
a time for all people to stand
To be judged by your deeds and actions
and the way you cared for this land

Bindi

The Aboriginal Artist

dedicated to my husband, Willie

I watch him paint, this man of art
with brush in hand as he works till dark.
He works with skill, each little mark
turns into beauty upon the bark.

He paints on shells as well as wood
sometimes I really wish I could.
He uses colours to make it bright:
there's RED and YELLOW, BLACK and WHITE.

These colours mean so much to him
as it depicts this country he was born in.
The markings too are of special means
as he puts them on to complete the scenes.

He paints each stroke with greatest ease
as he turns the wood into a masterpiece.
He does not hurry, he does not rush
he works on steady with the tiny brush.

Lena Adams

A Dream

I see you there
with a lovely smile.
I don't know what it is...
Lust? Love? Or is it a dream?

Can I have you?
Think not!
You're way beyond my reach.
I wish I could.

But that's just impossible
and the way it is has to be
so now I dream of what
could have been.

But I finally realized...
it's just a dream...

Lavinia Ahlers

Kate Oates

25

Point of View

I'm entitled to a point of view,
I'm allowed to have my say.
it may not sit well with all of you,
but I'm the writer, we'll do it my way.

Let's talk about the lot:
what's on people's minds.
The subjects are so many
like people; there are all different kinds.

What about smoking, sex and drugs
politics, religion and race?
Things that are mentioned at parties;
like how the country's now arse-about-face.

I don't wholly believe in the bible;
I reckon a lot of it's okay.
Too many cultures and people have died
hearing: "God is the only way!"

I wonder if you have experimented?
You know, smoked 'weed', or 'pot'?
So much for broadening horizons;
a closed society is all we've got.

And then there's the subject of sex:
what gender, who, what, where.
Everyone to their consenting own;
me, I'm just a square.

There's the thing on race and colour;
how leases extinguish Native Right.
Who owned the land before the government?
"It was nobody's." - Yeah right!

How many bow to the Queen?
Who will fight for her and her heirs?
How many have been to London
to see the queen who's supposedly theirs?

I thought all men were equal;
is that the dream of the poor and the few?
In this person eat person society
where money says: "I'm better than you."

I'm tired of being a slave,
and of asking for what's rightly mine.
If you're not in for good,
please leave, 'cause I'm still doing fine.

John Paiwan

26

Garry Namponan

28

Del Kendrick

Ghost Story

They say spirits roam the land
from the outback to the sea.
Whether they are here or not
they still scare the shit out of me.

Sitting around the campfire
hot coals reflect in the eye
and at any sudden movement
I'll jump so high I'll fly.

The hairyman, cleverman, featherfoot
could be there but out of sight.
All these friggin stories
will keep me awake tonight.

There are things you shouldn't do:
at night the whistling must stop.
If you call something up tonight
I'll faint - I'll surely drop!

With these creatures I don't need marijuana
with this fear I'm as high as a kite.
So please, no more bloody ghost stories
'cause I'll surely die of fright.

John Paiwan

30

Kathleen Davies

Beyond the Mist

How cruel life is
memories swirl in your brain
Like a myriad
of colors
Memories you'd like to forget
Hidings, Humiliation and Intimidation
roaring in your ears
Blocking out the present
fading to the past

What kind of person
do they grow up to be?
Chromers, Drunks or Speed Freaks
all in the name of the ultimate blackout
Blotting out visions
you kind of regret
The pictures keep coming
faster and faster
Please oh please
make me forget

Who am I?
I start to ask myself
Where do I want to be
a little down the creek?
What's going to happen if I
don't slow down
Start rowing the boat
to happier shores?

The fog is lifting
I can see the path
to brighter shores

Janelle Evans

chromers: paint-sniffers

Pain

Have you ever felt the pain
    of not knowing who you are
    of not knowing who you could tell
What are the thoughts
    going through your mind
    going through theirs
When does the horror
    stop giving you flashbacks
    stop giving you heartache
What did I do to deserve
    the hands on my body
    the hands in my space
Where are the emotions
    when the eyes are looking
    when the actions are over
Why are you hurting
    the innocent victims
    the innocent kin
How many more people
    feel the pain of your actions
    feel the pain inside their souls
Have you ever felt the pain
    of not knowing who you are
    of not knowing who to tell?

Janelle Evans

Brotherz

Two brothers have I
with many more cousins
Uncles and bunjis
and many more wazzams

The bros on the streets
the ones in the park
What do they do
when it's cold and it's dark

Sounds scary to me
when they start to hear voices
The poisons they've taken
leave them with no choices

There's bros in the can
whose ART shows ability
Seems quite a pity
they're in THAT facility

'Cause we need our bros
right here beside us
To show us the way
to help and to guide us

We don't need any more
sadness or sorrows
We must look ahead
for our tomorrows

Lots of healing
needs to take place
For the brotherz to stand up
for our once proud race

I'm not laughing or jeering
or having fun
I'm thinking of my nephews
and my sons

And what if you're single
and there's no way to cope
Would *you* step in
and give US some hope?

Our boys today, men of tomorrow
PLEASE don't bring us anymore sorrow
'Cause we love you all the men of our race
Who do you think we'd
get in your place?

Please help in the ways
you know that you can
And show our Gundoonoos
HOW TO BE A MAN!

Janelle Evens

33

34

Janelle Evans

Message to My Girlz

This message is for all the young girls
teenagers coming up in the world:
Respect yourself and your body
protect your sacredness with a waddy
Open your eyes to see the cheats
the conners, the liars offering treats
Don't go with them please, they're after no good
they'll say anything for your womanhood
Take your time to choose your mate
take it easy, go on a date
Look within for your identity
'cause there's plenty of time to lose your virginity
If he's a nice guy, he'll wait till you're ready
down the line, you may even go steady
Just leave it awhile and have a good think
don't wanna be bunjilbay or smell stink
'Cause the dangers are there if you play with fire
just tell him he won't die from desire
Tell him firmly or he won't believe
and then you'll find he won't leave
Look him in the eye and tell him NO
and that you want him to go
This message is for all the young girls:
cherish your diamonds and your pearls.

Janelle Evans

waddy - Australian Aboriginal fighting stick
bunjilbay - pregnant

My Grandfather's Story

Before time, going back in the early days
before it was called Old Mitchell River Mission
- that's back in my Dad's days
going back in the early days
the story I was told, from my Dad and my Uncles
about this whitefella
they used to call him old Frank Bowman
he was a missionary.
When settlers used to come from overseas
he went up to my mission, and set up camp there
at Old Mitchell River. He been there for a while
and got the people interacting with him.
He went in there
well, people were scared of white people back then, and he...
Everything was good there... he was supplying tobacco, tealeaf, portwine.
This story here I'm telling you, it's a true story.
It's related to my Granddad, my father's father
my Great Granddad
my old Granddad's name Ol' Willy Daphney.
Well, one day, it was Christmas day, everybody was there...
Beforehand my Granddad made a special lancewood spear
with a special bone in it, maybe a stingray bone.
Little did this whitefella know
my Granddad made that spear for him.

So Old Frank Bowman, he shouted all them old people
my granny, aunties, cousins, shouted them portwine, made em all drunk
- it was Christmas day.

Then my Granddad, and his wife, my Granny, and my Dad - he was roundabout fifteen,
they knew - there was a bad sign that there was going to be something bad happen on that day
so my Granddad, my Granny - my Dad's father and mother
they went down to this big lagoon not far from the camp
and, well, they set off there to that waterhole now
and my Granddad carried all these spears, that bundle of spears, and woomera

this was before rifles; there were only traditional weapons.
So one day he set up the camp
he heard strange noises - whipping, the sound of gunshots
'earing them singing out, their voices echoing across the ridges
and my Granddad knew there was trouble at the mission.

My Granddad ran out on the flats
he saw smoke, and people running, trying to protect themselves
from Bowman and his mob.
My Granddad seen them little kids running and crying
in a state of shock
- the people were all drunk when that incident took place -
my Granddad ran out in the open with the bundle of spears
and that lancewood spear, the one he made special
and that spear, it was made special for this fulla, Frank Bowman.

And on that same Christmas Day a woman was raped and killed.
And that creek there had no name
but now today it's called Christmas Creek
and everyone in Kowanyama knows that story.

Well all these things, my Dad took me out when I was small.
I witnessed all these burial sites, including my Granddad's burial site.
I witnessed - it was handed down to me as a child.

After that my Granddad showed himself, standing up with his spear
shaking it and waiting for Bowman to approach him.
My Granddad hid behind a big bloodwood tree
and Bowman came down, on his horse.
My Granddad jumped out from that tree
and Bowman's rifle was in the saddlebag
my Granddad shot Bowman straight through the head with that lancewood spear
no miss
Bowman was on a horse, tossing and weaving in the saddle,
and they couldn't pull that spear out from his head
no matter how hard they tried.
Bowman's troops came down, tried to pull that spear this way and that way

they couldn't pull it out
it was stuck in his brains, his skull.
So my Uncle told me
the troops couldn't help him
that spear gripped him like a vice.

So - some of my uncles told me - that they took after my Granddad, down to the lagoon
my Granddad told my Nanna and my father to run up to the ridges
and hide in a big hollow log, the kind that dingoes use to stuff wallaby carcasses in.
It stank, but my Grandmother tied a rag around my father's nose. They hid their tracks.
My grandfather took off to the waterhole
that was the only place he could hide
he broke off the stem of a waterlily, used it to breathe.
The troopers came down
they wondered how he could disappear so quick
my Uncle, Aunty, my nana mob told me they shot my granddad in the water
it was the only place he could be hiding, watching them from the waterlilies.
He got shot in the upper body
but he still hold himself...
I'm not sure about that.... but he died, that day.

Now today that story's been handed down
they are very grateful for what my granddad did
to build a better life
a better community.
Today Old Bowman, they buried him with that spear
a couple of years back they reopened, put a monument there
a big plaque, telling the history there.
This one Rotland Station, Rotland Plains
five miles out of Kowanyama
they opened that, it's on the ridge.
Station here, got the yard not far, there's writing there now about my grandfather
speared that Bowman.
They changed that name from Old Mitchell River Mission which they call today
Kowanyama.
You know why they call it Kowanyama?
The Place of Many, Many Waters - too rich, dry season, wet season

that's all my Dad's country
my tribe, up in Kowanyama, the Kokobera tribe
they're the property mob for this country.
They got other members of the tribe; Kokomindjena, Kunjen tribe, Kokobera
there's another one there, but I don't know.

When they went up to reopen that place of Bowman the Murris said
"Why you open that place?" but they still show him respect
but people said "You should open up a place for Ol' Willy Daphney."
But when people go up there they've gotta ask permission.

Harry Daphney

Robbie Paul

40

Bindi

My Incarceration

I'm thinking of you all the time
I've been convicted of a crime
a two year sentence
is hard to accept
as the judge read my conviction
I stood there and wept.

My little man was present
he started to cry.
The thought of being apart:
I contemplated whether to die.

After some counselling
I've had time to find
a way to get rid of
the thought of death on my mind.
Now Christmas is close
and I'll still be in here
but I hope to see you guys
in the New Year.

Kevin Brown

Grandmother

My grandmother, do you think she's unsightly or ugly?
Is she nothing more than an irritation?
Or a source of frustration and physical discomfort;
maybe even mental frustration?

But what do you really see
when you gaze into her dark brown eyes?
Do you perceive the reflection of your own exquisite spirit?
What do you feel, when she sings you a bedtime lullaby?
Do you feel the heartbeat of her enchanted sacred love for you?

Tell me:
what do you think of my grandmother?

Letitia Scott

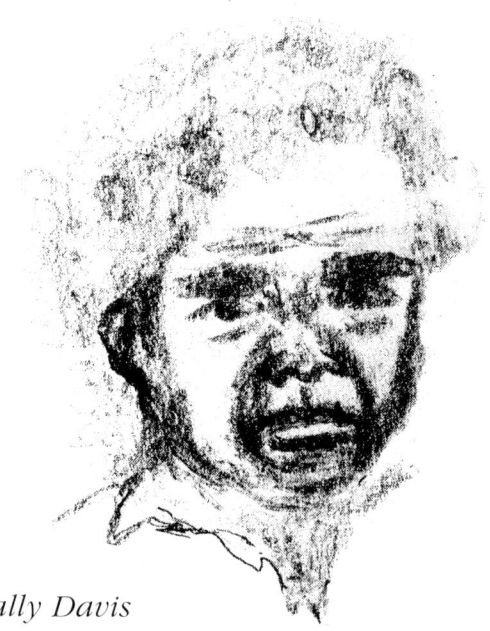

Sally Davis

Alone

Near a bridge there stood a man
He carried an old rusted can
Upon his head there laid a hat
And near the bridge the old man sat.

He started to whistle an old tune
Because he knew something would be arriving soon
And when the old man turned around
The smile he had turned to a frown.

But then at last a cool breeze came
And on his face a smile again
He shut his eyes as tight as he could
And at the bridge the old man stood.

He held out his arms and waited awhile
And grew an even bigger smile
A ghostly figure took his hand
And directed him across the land

Until he was up above
With his only one true love!

Bonnie Cavanagh

At the End of the Day

(song of the elders)

You took me under your wings
and you changed my view of me
you led me in your ways
you told me what to do and say
and you kept me to this day.

But at the end of the day
I needed to be me
I wanted respect, and my old ways
to have my say
at the end of the day.

I lived here with you
and followed all your rules
replaced my lores
gave you my life's all
to do with as you pleased.

But at the end of the day
I needed to be me
I wanted respect, and my old ways
to have my say
at the end of the day.

I'm a sorrowful version
of a once-proud vision.
Your way of life
robbed my soul, my place
and I live in silent disgrace.

Still, at the end of the day
I need to be me
I want respect, for my way
to have my say
at the end of the day.

Sally Davis

Sally Davis

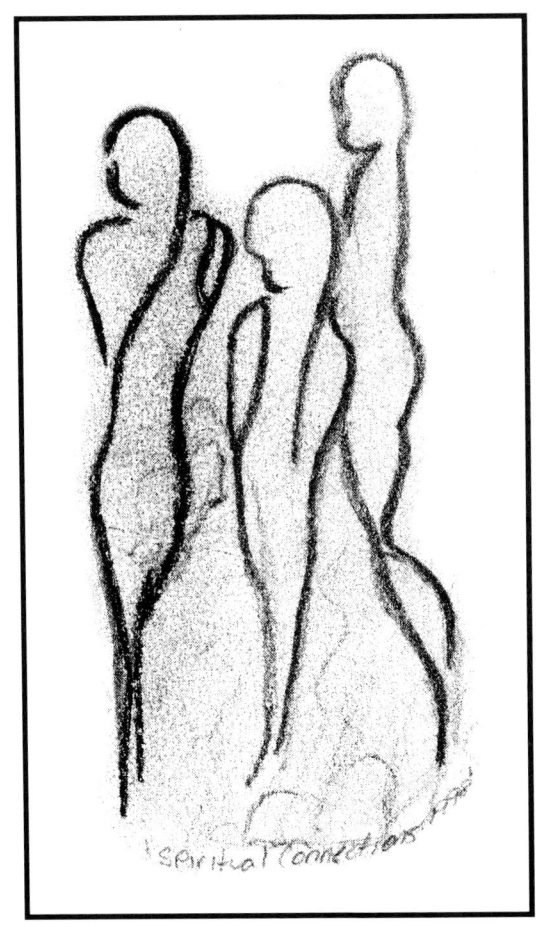

"Spiritual Connections"

Sally Davis

Another's Child

I came into this world not knowing
I came into this world full of loving

I came into my mother's arms from another
because there was no other.
My father let my mother watch me grow.
I came a daughter to my parents
a sister to me balas
then my mother took another
and she became me sister

I have never tasted my mother's milk
but have tasted her love, strength and anger.

My mother watched me become a mother
and with love I gave my own.

I see this now, it happen a lot
me being adopted and reluctant to say
conflict arises and I am reminded
I am not an unwanted
I am the strength that bond two families.

I was told not by my mother
but by another
I came from a sister of my mother
my kupi mother became my aunt
my aunt sister became my mother.

Betrayed I felt
but you see
when I see my mother
I see me.

Elthies Kris

Secrets

Secrets
those little things we keep hidden away
secrets
they fill our minds from day to day

Secrets
they slither and creep around our minds
secrets
they try to crawl out, from time to time

Secrets
concealed, secluded, shrouded
secrets
never to be revealed

Secrets
made during the passion between two people
secrets
hurtful, false, fabricated and deceitful

Secrets
whispered softly in the witching hour
secrets
too many can make the heart sour

Secrets
you need to be quiet; don't let them hear
secrets
be careful, they don't care who is near

Robert Salt

Robbie Paul

49

Funny How

Funny how things get muddle, in a funny kind of way
Funny how we answer, when we weren't supposed to say

Funny how the answer came, when it wasn't there at all
Funny how a joke was told, and yet it made us bawl

Funny how the noise was loud, in a silent atmosphere
Funny how we screamed it out, yet whispered in our ear

Funny how I think about, these and many more
Funny how we memories, which are definitely not a chore

They are a question in a thought! I guess you could say
Funny how we memories, that flow from day to day

A little bit confusing, in any situation
Funny how we memories, that need no explanation

Glenda Power

Me, My Shadow and I

I am a shadow of my shadow,
I follow my shadow and me around.
Dark and maybe handsome,
Spreading gracefully across the ground.

People walk all over me,
not that I've a choice.
Sometimes I feel like saying something,
but I haven't any voice.

Me and my shadow are quite busy
going here and there;
even though I tag along
they couldn't give a care.

I must admit; I'm very quiet,
I never say a word.
Only my shadow tags along
like a real nerd.
Me has everything to say,
in every situation.
Sometimes I wish that I was me
but it's only infatuation.

Now I sit and take a look, at
me, my shadow and I.
And I think to myself: I'm really me;
there's never been an I.

I is just a part of me,
and we're just one of a kind.
So it's really me and my shadow
that were here all the time.

Glenda Power

Winter

It's here at last
My favourite time of year
Frosty mornings, dew on grass
Summer's gone and lowers the cheer.

Steaming hot showers
Cold fingers, cold toes
Relax now, mellow
Winter takes away your woes.

Outside smell the cool air
Crisp and clear
Foggy breath, clean lungs
Conditions that calm all your fears.

Warm jackets, woollen gloves
In dad's kitchen, a soup in a pot
The feeling of family warmth is around me
Stoke the fire place with logs, make it nice and hot.

Pack away the swimmers
Pack away that fan
Pack away the sunscreen
Say goodbye to your tan.

People say winter's bad
Colds and flu, here they come
People raving, going mad
Lay the blanket out, play games, what fun.

I smile, you see, on my lounge
Reading my favourite book in hand
Page to page takes away my frown
As the story takes me away to a magical land.

A video, a crackling fire
Your family by your side
You can have your hot weather
Winter takes me on my dream ride.

Alison Salt

53

Del Kendrick

Biographies

ALISON SALT

was born in Brewarrina, NSW and spent most of her childhood in red dirt country of outback Australia. She became a teacher in 1996. Currently residing in Dubbo, Alison largely focuses on raising her six children with her husband Zeke. They both play a large part in the Dubbo Westside Junior Rugby League Club. Alison is currently studying for a Master degree in Social Science (Aboriginal Studies).

(BINDI) BELYNDA WAUGH

is a visual artist of Jiman and Bundjalung descent. She established Yarwun Pottery eight years ago (near Gladstone) and also works as an illustrator and painter. "Within my art I like to explore the indigenous way of living within our environment and the importance of it to all people."

BONNIE CAVANAGH

comes from Broadford in Victoria. Still at school, she has been writing poems just for fun since she was ten years old, as her interests lie mainly in sport. With a few comments by readers of her writings she thought she might enter her poem into the Black Ink Writing Competition, where it was selected for this anthology.

COLIN J DAISY (1954 - 2003)

was taken as a young boy to the Boys Home on Palm Island. During his adult years Colin travelled extensively throughout Australia, learning the language and culture of his people. It was in prison that Colin learned to read and write, developing his natural talent as a storyteller and poet. Colin passed away in January 2003.

DEL KENDRICK

is from the Jirrabal clan of North Queensland, and graduated from Cairns TAFE with a Diploma in Visual Arts in 2002. She has pursued a career in Beauty Therapy for 20 years, this being her first love. In 2002 as Gigoroo (Beautiful) Designs, Del participated in a workshop on jewellery design, and was successful at the 2003 February Jewellery Expo in Sydney.

DENNIS FISHER

was raised at Cherbourg Mission in Queensland but made Melbourne his home. He is an actor, did the Advanced Certificate in Koori Art & Design and is currently completing his Diploma of Arts (Professional Writing & Editing). Dennis is passionate in his desire to help the wider community to understand more, and hopes to use his acting, writing and design skills to that end.

ELTHIES (ELLA) KRIS

was born and raised on beautiful Thursday Island in Tamwoy Town, her mother from Darnley and father from St Pauls (Moa Island). She lives and works on Thursday Island and her writing comes from when she lived in Townsville for 12 months and was homesick every day thinking of the families, the sea and the simple the way of life.

ELLEN GO-SAM

was born in Gayndah in 1954. She spent her childhood years in Baralaba, Central Queensland. She won a scholarship to complete her secondary schooling. From a very early age she had a great love of nature, music and poetry. She was married at eighteen, and has never stopped writing throughout her life.

GARRY NAMPONAN

is part of an Aplech Wik Ngathan family at Aurukun Community in Cape York Peninsula, son of an eminent artist. His family company used to produce screen-printed textiles and lino block prints. He practises as a sculptor, painter, screen-printer and illustrator. His wood and cast bronze sculptures have been exhibited in Brisbane and he is represented in the travelling exhibition <u>Native Title Business</u>.

GLENDA POWER

is a member of the Paul family of eleven from Bowen. She attended school for eight years and her favourite subject was English. She loved to write stories about things her friends would say and do. Those short stories gradually became poems that she continues to write today. "I guess the novelty never wore off," she said.

55

HARRY DAPHNEY

was born at Townsville in 1965, while his parents were living at Palm Island after droving cattle. He went to school at Palm. His dad, an Aboriginal man from Mitchell River Mission (now Kowanyama) met his Chinese mother at Normanton. Harry has also lived at Kowanyama and Normanton, and was fostered by white parents in Mount Isa.

JANELLE EVANS

was born in Brisbane in 1970, of the Wadja tribe of Woorabinda. She was taken from her mother at the age of 9 months and her mother was allowed to get her 4 year old daughter back upon her marriage to a white man. Janelle has been a radio broadcaster, public speaker and Aboriginal rights activist. She began her career in radio at fourteen with the Townsville Aboriginal Islander Media Association. She is a mother of five and lives in Townsville.

JAQUANNA ELLIOT

was born in Dubbo NSW and grew up in South Australia, her identity kept from her until, nine years ago, she became aware of her indigenous heritage and met her natural mother who told her of her tribe, the Dunghutti "river people" in Kempsey NSW. Jaquanna has resided in four states. She took up painting and sculpture in 1999 and would like to use her gift to help her people.

JOHN LEWIS CLARK

was born in Warrnambool, Western Victoria, in 1953, with family ties to the Gunditjmara nation. A writer and visual artist, he attended Framlingham Aboriginal Settlement school before moving to Gippsland, Melbourne and now Geelong. He has worked as a labourer, and in various Victorian Aboriginal organisations. His short stories and poetry have been published by Penguin, and in Across Country (ABC Books), Yarmbler Magazine and Australian Short Stories. He studied Koori art at the Geelong College of TAFE.

56

JOHN W PAIWAN

is of Australian dugong blood and lives in Townsville,. He says, "Thankyou for reading my words. A big hello to my family . I wrote 'Ghost Story' whilst on a nature camp with students out of Sydney. I wrote 'Point of View' as a frustrated reaction to dealing with government services. I may not be much, only a black fella, but my mind soars and I smile."

KATE OATES

was born at Penrith NSW and grew up there and in Armidale on a small family property. From 2 years old her Aboriginal Nan told her she had art in her and she started scribbling as a small child to keep quiet in church. She has just graduated with a Bachelor of Communications Design at JCU Townsville and is starting out as an illustrator and designer.

KATHLEEN DAVIES

is of Wiradjuri descent. She started writing and painting as a young child, and since then has won several awards for her poems and paintings. She is currently represented in the travelling exhibition Billy Cans. She has worked as a ranger in Aboriginal communities in Central Australia, and was involved in the establishment of the Ulugundahi Art and Culture Centre in MacLean, Northern NSW. Kathleen teaches at Lawrence Primary School.

KEVIN BROWN

was born in Townsville in 1962. He has seven sisters and eight brothers. He tried his hand at poetry whilst in prison, where his mind got clear from all the bad toxins which are available on the outside. He just wants one message to get across: "Prison is no place to find out the ability that everyone has within them. Find it and use it to help someone to achieve a goal too".

LAVINIA R AHLERS

was born in Cairns and grew up in Coen. She was looking at art and poetry at an early age at school and got really interested in art and started doing some painting. She says, "I encourage other young people to put what they can do to good use and even if they find at first they can't do it, at least try".

57

LENA ADAMS

was born at Old Mapoon, Cape York Peninsula, in 1949, of the Thanikutti Yapangathi people, and has since lived in many places in North Queensland. Her interests are reading, writing, listening to stories, gardening and photography. She has just graduated with an Advanced Diploma in Indigenous Studies (Communications) from James Cook University, Townsville.

Biographies

LETITIA SCOTT

is descended from Arente and Beeru people. She began life in the slums of Woolloomooloo, trained and worked as a nurse in Victoria, and now her retirement in Townsville is filled with voluntary work. She was always involved in politics and was inspired to write by friends Kath Walker, Judith Wright and Maureen Watson. This is the first of her many poems to be published.

LINDSAY OHL

was born and raised at Gogango, west of Rockhampton. He is strong on bush food and medicine, makes and uses all types of artifacts, and plays the didgeridoo. He has been scribbling for a few years, and this is his first publication. "Lost" was read by Mick Dodson at the Reconciliation Working Together Conference in Mackay, 1998.

MALCOLM BALLY

was born in Coen in 1960, of Kaanju and Oolkulo parents. During childhood he travelled with his parents and younger brother and sisters throughout Cape York, working on cattle stations. They lived at Coen and Laura then, after he lost his mother, moved to Hope Vale north east of Cooktown where they were adopted into foster homes. He now has a family of his own and expects to be at Hope Vale forever.

MARIAN J GO SAM

was born at Atherton FNQ where she currently resides. Her poems have been published in Dancing in Light (International Library of Poetry 2002, Editor's Choice Award) and Poet's Reflections 2002 (Arrow Publishing) and she is planning to publish her own in the near future.

REBECCA EDWARDS

was born into an Anglo-Celtic family in Batlow NSW in 1969. She grew up in Nambucca Heads, the Northern Territory, Papua New Guinea, Nauru and Japan. She is a poet and visual artist who has exhibited, taught, and had three books published: Eating the Experience (Metro Press 1994) Scar Country (UQP 2000) and Holiday Coast Medusa (Five Islands Press 2002). While living in Townsville she became involved with the Black Ink Project as part of the judging panel for the inaugural writing and Illustrating Awards which were the beginning of this anthology.

ROBBIE PAUL

is also part of the family of eleven from Bowen, and the father of two. After working in the meat processing industry and practising art as a hobby, painting local murals and exhibiting paintings, he enrolled in the Bachelor of Communications Design course at James Cook University, Townsville, and has just graduated. He is now working as a graphic designer and illustrator.

ROBERT SALT

is originally from Brewarrina, NSW. He is currently living and working in Dubbo. He has written a wide range of poetry on various topics and is about to complete his first novel. His mother's language group is the Murrawarri.

SALLY DAVIS

has lived all her life in the small town of Tolga, North Queensland. It boasts not only the Great Dividing Range, the Barron River, rural acreage, forests and blue skies but also legends and tragedies of her people's people. Sally began scribbling words on paper at the age of twelve.

(YUNKE) AARON ELLIOT

was born 33 years ago at Yarrabah Aboriginal Community not far from Cairns. He started writing poetry in 1993 at Lotus Glen Prison and continued at Stuart Creek. He now lives in suburban Townsville. When writing he likes peace and quiet and looking at the landscape.

60

Bindi

THE BLACK INK PROJECT

Black Ink is an Indigenous community writing, illustrating and publishing project based in Townsville and Thuringowa, Far North Queensland. The idea is to find storytellers, writers and artists, and build skills to enable them to create books, through workshops and individual mentorship.

Black Ink aims to publish contemporary books especially for Indigenous children and young people to read, picture story books, fiction and non-fiction; illustrated biographies of local people, and some traditional stories.

Black Ink recognises the importance of Indigenous community languages and aims to support individuals and groups in their diverse publishing projects including books and audio and visual and digital media.

Copyright in stories and artwork belongs to the people who create them, and families or communities will be considered too if appropriate when paying fees or royalties to copyright owners.

Black Ink would like to hear from people who are writers or illustrators or have stories to tell. There is a mailing list for the occasional newsletter and for news of forthcoming titles - please send your name and address.

CONTACT
The Black Ink Project
Yalga-binbi Institute for Community Development
190 Hervey's Range Road (behind Shalom Christian College) Condon
phone 07 4773 5077 fax 07 4773 5307
PO Box 217, Thuringowa, QLD 4817

blackinkybi@ozemail.com.au